Space-ology

Investigating
ASTEROIDS

by Ellen Lawrence

Consultant:
Josh Barker
Space Communications Team
National Space Centre
Leicester, United Kingdom

BEARPORT PUBLISHING

New York, New York

Credits

Cover, © solarseven/Shutterstock; 4, © Frank Zullo/Science Photo Library; 5, © Alin Brotea/Shutterstock, © I. Pilon/Shutterstock, and © MSSA/Shutterstock; 6, © Action Sports Photography/Shutterstock; 7, © Ruby Tuesday Books; 8, © Jon Hicks/Getty Images; 9, © ImageFlow/Shutterstock, © Horvats/Shutterstock, and © I. Pilon/Shutterstock; 10, Public Domain; 11, © John Hopkins University Applied Physics Laboratory/Science Photo Library; 12, Public Domain; 13, © ustas7777777/Shutterstock and © Hulton Archive/Getty Images; 14, © solarseven/Shutterstock; 15, © Detlev Van Ravenswaay/Science Photo Library; 16, © NASA; 17, © NASA; 18, © Adwo/Shutterstock, © I. Pilon/Shutterstock, and © Dmitri Gruzdev/Shutterstock; 19, © Stocktrek Images Inc/Alamy; 20, © Mark Garlick/Science Photo Library; 21, © Jan Kaliciak/Shutterstock; 22, © Dan Kosmayer/Shutterstock, © Big Foot Productions/Shutterstock, © Palokha Tetiana/Shutterstock, © Zovteva/Shutterstock, © Daniel Chetroni/Shutterstock, and © Ruth Owen Books; 23TL, © Dabarti CGI/Shutterstock; 23TC, © turtix/Shutterstock; 23TR, © Best-Backgrounds/Shutterstock; 23BL, © NASA/James Blair; 23BC, © Stanslavs/Shutterstock; 23BR, © Madhourse/Shutterstock.

Publisher: Kenn Goin
Senior Editor: Joyce Tavolacci
Creative Director: Spencer Brinker
Photo Researcher: Ruth Owen Books

Library of Congress Cataloging-in-Publication Data

Names: Lawrence, Ellen, 1967– author.
Title: Investigating asteroids / by Ellen Lawrence.
Description: New York, New York : Bearport Publishing, [2019] | Series:
    Space-ology | Includes bibliographical references
    and index.
Identifiers: LCCN 2018050777 (print) | LCCN 2018051451 (ebook) | ISBN
    9781642802474 (ebook) | ISBN 9781642801781 (library)
Subjects: LCSH: Asteroids—Juvenile literature. | Space flight to
    asteroids—Juvenile literature. | Space mining—Juvenile literature. |
    Eros (Asteroid)—Juvenile literature.
Classification: LCC QB651 (ebook) | LCC QB651 .L385 2019 (print) | DDC
    523.44—dc23
LC record available at https://lccn.loc.gov/2018050777

For more information, write to Bearport Publishing Company, Inc., 45 West 21st Street, Suite 3B, New York, New York 10010. Printed in the United States of America.

10 9 8 7 6 5 4 3 2 1

Contents

A Terrifying Discovery 4

What Are Asteroids? 6

A Near Miss 8

Asteroid Explorer 10

Up Close with Eros 12

Space Crash! 14

A Mission to Bennu 16

Mining Asteroids 18

Water from Space Rocks 20

Science Lab 22

Science Words 23

Index 24

Read More 24

Learn More Online 24

About the Author 24

A Terrifying Discovery

One night in June 2004, three scientists were looking for **asteroids**.

Using powerful **telescopes**, they spotted one that was about 1,000 feet (305 m) long.

That's the same length as three football fields!

The scientists tracked the asteroid's pathway as it hurtled through space.

Their **data** showed that it might collide with Earth on April 13, 2029!

starry night sky

telescope

asteroid

Earth

The scientists called the asteroid Apophis. They named it after the ancient Egyptian god of darkness and destruction.

What Are Asteroids?

Asteroids are large space rocks.

They can be as small as a car— or as big as a mountain.

There are millions of asteroids orbiting the Sun in a ring called the asteroid belt.

Sometimes, however, the giant rocks crash into each other.

Then, one might get knocked outside of the asteroid belt and come flying toward Earth!

If the asteroid Apophis hit Earth, it would make a **crater** 2.7 miles (4.3 km) wide. It would destroy everything within miles of the crash site.

This crater was made by an asteroid that hit Earth 50,000 years ago.

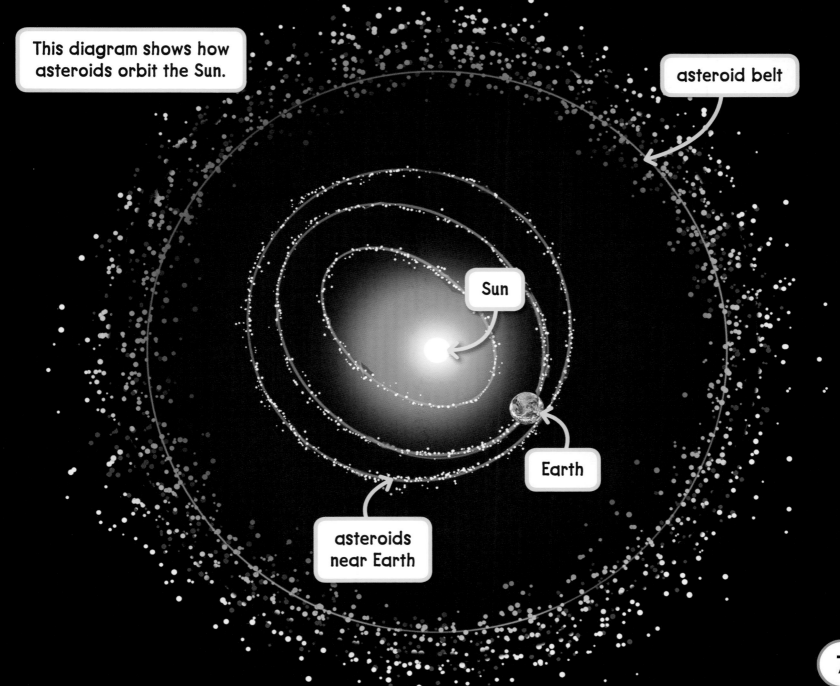

This diagram shows how asteroids orbit the Sun.

asteroid belt

Sun

Earth

asteroids near Earth

A Near Miss

Once scientists discovered Apophis, they got to work tracking it.

They uploaded details of the asteroid's space voyage to a powerful computer.

The computer figured out what the asteroid's orbit would be for the next 100 years.

Luckily, the data showed that Apophis would not hit Earth—but it would fly very close!

a scientist watching for asteroids

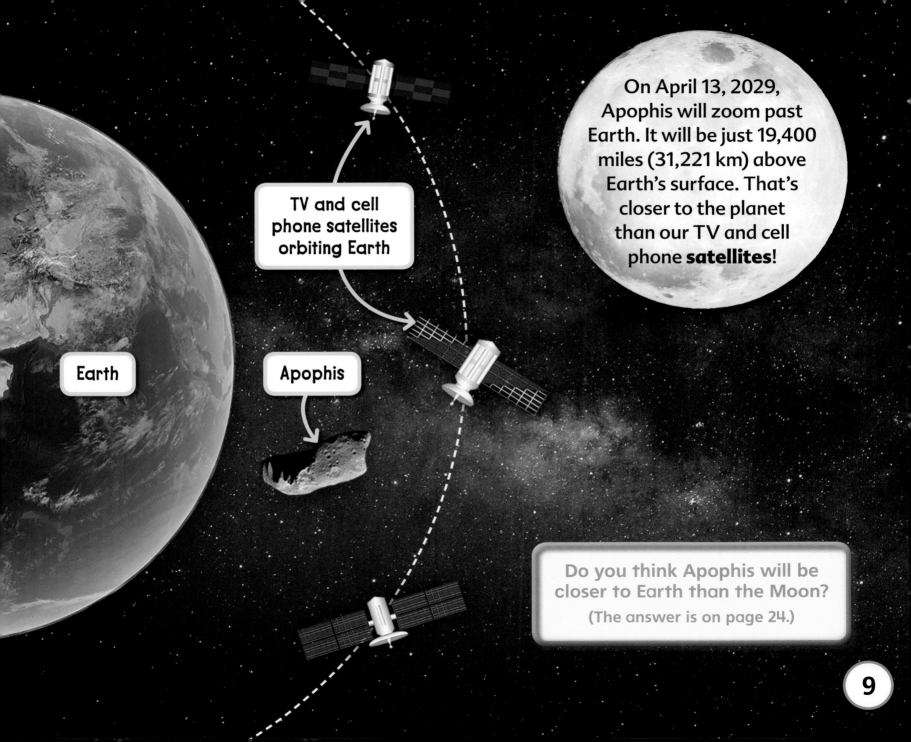

TV and cell phone satellites orbiting Earth

On April 13, 2029, Apophis will zoom past Earth. It will be just 19,400 miles (31,221 km) above Earth's surface. That's closer to the planet than our TV and cell phone **satellites**!

Earth

Apophis

Do you think Apophis will be closer to Earth than the Moon?

(The answer is on page 24.)

Asteroid Explorer

Day and night, scientists keep watch for dangerous asteroids.

They also send spacecraft to these rocky giants to learn about them.

In 1996, **NASA** (National Aeronautics and Space Administration) launched the spacecraft *NEAR Shoemaker*.

It flew by an asteroid called Mathilde, taking hundreds of photos.

Then, in 2000, it began to orbit a large asteroid named Eros.

NEAR Shoemaker **on a rocket**

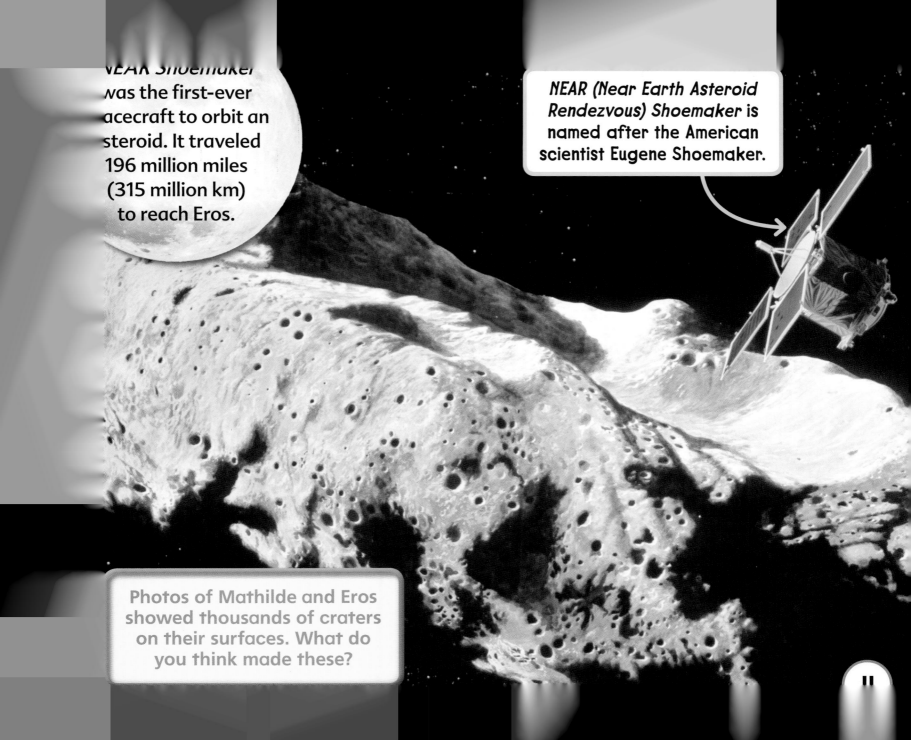

Up Close with Eros

After orbiting Eros for about a year, *NEAR Shoemaker*'s final adventure began.

The spacecraft flew closer to the asteroid.

As it did, it sent photos of Eros's surface back to Earth.

Then, the spacecraft landed on the asteroid!

Its mission was finally over.

photos taken by *NEAR Shoemaker*

Mathilde

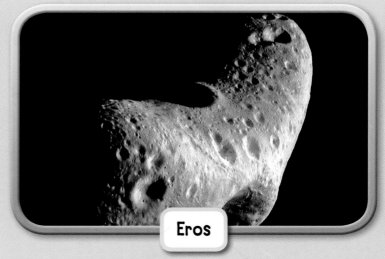

Eros

NEAR Shoemaker Mission Data

- The spacecraft took 160,000 images of Eros.
- Eros has about 100,000 craters on its surface—a result of collisions with other asteroids.
- Some of the craters are miles wide.
- Eros is also covered with giant rocks and rubble from crashes with other asteroids.

NEAR Shoemaker and Eros could be flying through space together for billions of years!

his illustration shows *NEAR Shoemaker* out to land on Eros.

Space Crash!

If a deadly asteroid is heading for Earth, could scientists knock it off course?

In 2022, the DART spacecraft will fly to the asteroids Didymos and Didymoon.

Traveling at high speed, DART will crash into Didymoon and, hopefully, push it off course.

If the test works, it means a spacecraft could be used to protect Earth from asteroids!

an illustration of an asteroid crash

A Mission to Bennu

In July 2020, the *OSIRIS-REx* spacecraft will visit an asteroid named Bennu.

OSIRIS-REx will hover just above the asteroid's surface.

Then, in just five seconds, it will collect rock samples to see what Bennu is made of.

Finally, the samples will be blasted back to Earth.

OSIRIS-REx

rocket

OSIRIS-REx ready for launch

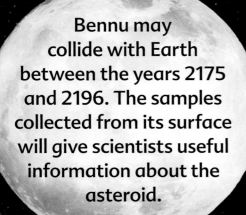

Bennu may collide with Earth between the years 2175 and 2196. The samples collected from its surface will give scientists useful information about the asteroid.

OSIRIS-REx

The spacecraft's robotic arm will grab the samples.

Bennu

Asteroids may be very useful to humans in the future. How do you think they could be used?

Mining Asteroids

Asteroids aren't only made of rock.

They also contain valuable metals such as iron, titanium, and even gold.

Some scientists think it's possible to collect these metals from asteroids.

Then, the metals can be sent to Earth and used there.

These pieces of rock came from asteroids. They all contain metal.

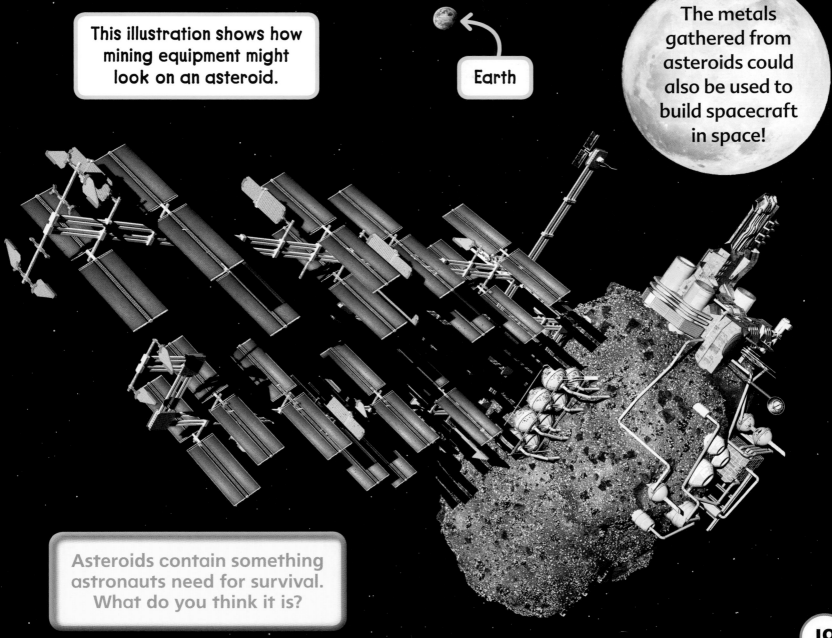

This illustration shows how mining equipment might look on an asteroid.

Earth

The metals gathered from asteroids could also be used to build spacecraft in space!

Asteroids contain something astronauts need for survival. What do you think it is?

Water from Space Rocks

In the future, astronauts may fly to Mars or to other distant places.

They will need water for drinking and growing food.

Water is heavy, so it's difficult to transport into space.

Scientists think that many asteroids contain water.

The asteroid water could be collected and then sent to Mars or other faraway places!

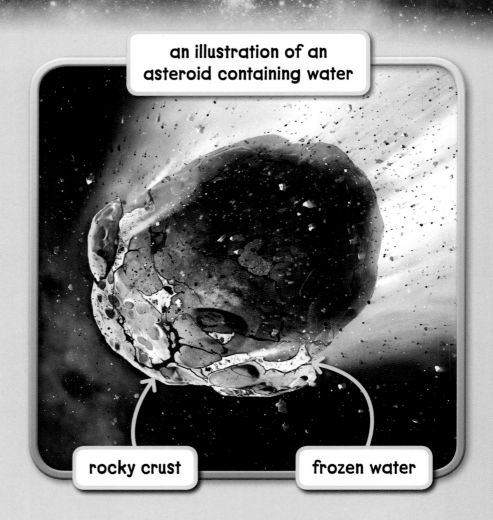

an illustration of an asteroid containing water

rocky crust

frozen water

This illustration shows what a fuel station orbiting Earth might look like.

One day, the water from asteroids could also be used to make fuel for spacecraft.

Science Lab

Be a Crater Investigator!

When an asteroid hits another asteroid or a planet, it makes a crater. Let's investigate!

You will need:
- A large metal baking pan
- Enough flour to fill the baking pan
- Objects for asteroids, for example, a marble, small rock, tennis ball, or baseball
- Measuring tape
- A notebook and pen

1. Place the baking pan on the ground outside. Fill it with flour and smooth the surface so it's flat.

2. Take one of the asteroid objects. Stand over the baking pan and drop the object into the flour from waist height.

3. Measure the size of the object and the crater it makes and record the measurements in your notebook.

4. Look for flour that has been thrown from the crater. Measure how far from the crater it landed. Material that is thrown from a crater is called ejecta.

5. Smooth out the flour and repeat the investigation with the other objects. Make sure you drop each object from the same height. Record your measurements.

- *Which object made the largest crater?*

- *Which object threw ejecta, or flour, farthest from its crater?*

Science Words

asteroids (AS-ter-roydz) large rock and metal objects that orbit the Sun

crater (KRAY-tur) a large, bowl-shaped hole in the ground

data (DAY-tuh) information, often in the form of numbers

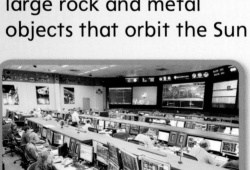

NASA (NAS-ah) a group of scientists and experts in the United States who study space and spacecraft

satellites (SAT-uh-lites) spacecraft or other objects that circle Earth or other planets

telescopes (TEL-uh-scopes) instruments or machines used for looking at space

Index

Apophis 5, 6, 8–9
asteroid belt 6–7
Bennu 16–17
craters 6, 11, 13, 22
DART 14–15

Didymoon 14–15
Didymos 14–15
Eros 10–11, 12–13
Mathilde 10–11, 12
mining asteroids 18–19

NEAR Shoemaker 10–11, 12–13
OSIRIS-REx 16–17
satellites 9
telescopes 4–5, 8
water on asteroids 20–21

Read More

Dickmann, Nancy. *Asteroids, Meteors, and Comets (Space: Facts and Figures)*. New York: Rosen (2019).

Lawrence, Ellen. *Comets, Meteors, and Asteroids: Voyagers of the Solar System (Zoom Into Space)*. New York: Ruby Tuesday (2014).

Rathburn, Betsy. *Asteroids (Space Science)*. Minnetonka, MN: Bellwether (2019).

Learn More Online

To learn more about asteroids, visit
www.bearportpublishing.com/space-ology

About the Author

Ellen Lawrence lives in the United Kingdom and fully admits to being a huge space geek! While researching and writing this series, she loved watching interviews with astronauts and spine-tingling launch countdowns.

Answer for Page 9

The Moon is 238,855 miles (384,400 km) from Earth. Apophis will be much closer to Earth than the Moon.